PUFFIN BOOKS

History Through Objects

Jeans

The stuff of American History

Régine Van Damme

History Through Objects

Jeans

The stuff of American History

Translated by Patrick White
Illustrated by Giampiero Caiti

PUFFIN BOOKS

PUFFIN BOOKS

Published by the Penguin Group
Penguin Books Ltd, 27 Wrights Lane, London W8 5TZ, England
Penguin Books USA Inc., 375 Hudson Street, New York, New York 10014, USA
Penguin Books Australia Ltd, Ringwood, Victoria, Australia
Penguin Books Canada Ltd, 10 Alcorn Avenue, Toronto, Ontario, Canada M4V 3B2
Penguin Books (NZ) Ltd, 182–190 Wairau Road, Auckland 10, New Zealand

Penguin Books Ltd, Registered Offices: Harmondsworth, Middlesex, England

First published by Casterman 1991
Published simultaneously in Viking and Puffin 1995
1 3 5 7 9 10 8 6 4 2

Filmset in Linotron Bembo by
Rowland Phototypesetting Limited, Bury St Edmunds, Suffolk

Made and printed in Singapore

Photograph Credits

All photographs of jeans are by Jean-Michel Labat © Casterman.
From the Levi's collection: pages 13, 19h and m, 27h, 32h, 42, 44.
Roger-Viollet: pages 14–15, 15hd, 16b, 18–19, 22–23, 28, 31, 35b.
J-L. Charmet: page 17.
Christophe L.: pages 21, 36b, 37, 38b, 39.
Or Information: page 27b.
Walt Disney: page 29.
DITE: page 32b.
D.R.: pages 35h, 36h, 40b.
Magnum: page 38h.

For Gwen and Antoine

Contents

Trousers built to last

Today almost all of us pull on a pair of jeans at some time. But how many of us realize that the story of jeans is closely tied up with the history of the United States? In fact jeans came about by chance, when an American pioneer in search of a strong pair of trousers happened to meet an immigrant from Central Europe out to make his fortune. That meeting resulted in the invention of a garment which is now worn all over the world.

A stitch-by-stitch guide

Apart from a couple of minor details, the classic style of jeans has not changed much since they were invented in the middle of the nineteenth century. At the time they were called cut-off dungarees and were worn with braces. They are still made from the same strong cotton fabric, although this was originally brown in colour (the switch to blue occurred in 1858). Traditional jeans are available in a range of waist sizes and leg measurements but their distinguishing features remain: five pockets, a fly with metal buttons, orange stitching to match the copper of the rivets, and an imitation-leather patch sewn on to the waist.

Not all the rivets used in the original design have been kept. The rivet at the crotch was removed in 1933 as it was causing problems for cattlemen, who liked to warm themselves by kneeling close to the campfire in the evenings! And the rivets on the back pockets were done away with in 1937 after complaints from headmasters that their classroom seats were being worn down too quickly for their liking . . .

In 1870 a tailor had the idea of replacing the seams at the corners of the pockets and at the crotch with copper rivets to make the jeans even tougher at these points of greatest stress. He couldn't afford to patent his invention, and so instead he went into partnership with the inventor of jeans two years later.

Good looks and a good label

With their wide waist and loose fit over the thighs, jeans gave the workers who originally wore them the comfort and strength they needed for heavy work.

The tab is the most recent change made to jeans, and was added in 1936. This small dark red label (0.5 cm by 1.5 cm) was machined into the seam of the right-hand back pocket, and carried on it in white letters the name of the original brand: Levi's.

In 1873 jeans grew wings on the back pockets, the wings of the Rocky Mountain eagle. A symbol of freedom, they take the form of two curves of orange stitching.

In 1886 jeans acquired some advertising space with the addition of the patch. It shows two horses being urged on by two men with whips as they try in vain to tear apart a pair of jeans.

The patch also gives information on the waist size of the trousers (W followed by a number), the leg measurement (L followed by a number), the design (501), and the quality of the fabric (XX meaning that it is extra strong).

LeVi's

Profession: travelling salesman

A hard-working and resourceful man of Bavarian extraction, Levi Strauss's story is one that could have happened only in America. In 1853, when he was twenty-four years old, he landed in San Francisco with gold on his mind and intent on making his fortune. But the gold-mine he made for himself was built with a sewing needle rather than a pickaxe.

From Genoa to jeans

The term jeans is derived from Genoese, and was first used in 1567. It referred to a fabric produced in Genoa in Italy for making sailors' trousers. However, the serge fabric from which Levi Strauss made his jeans in 1853 came from Nîmes in France. Manufactured for ships' sails and tarpaulins for covering wagons, it was known for being cheap and very strong. Encouraged by the demand from overseas markets, and in particular from North America, the makers of the textile from Nîmes set up shops in Genoa, which was then one of the most important centres of trade in the world. Later denim (a type of serge whose name comes from the French 'de Nîmes' meaning 'from Nîmes') found its way to the New World, only to return to Europe some 200 years later in the form of blue jeans, the teenager's essential fashion item.

A woven fabric is always made from two threads: a warp thread (vertical) and a weft thread (horizontal). A slightly different method is used for denim, with the weft thread passing successively under and over the warp thread in a diagonal configuration. This is known as a 'twill weave' and is what gives denim its great strength.

The port of Genoa in 1882.

Nîmes has been one of the biggest centres for textile production in Europe since the Middle Ages.

Another feature of indigo-dyed denim is that it fades gradually. This happens because only the surface of the thread is coloured during the dyeing process. The weft thread preserves its original white colour.

Blue is the colour

Denim is a hard-wearing fabric but its natural colour, ecru, means that it must be dyed a dark colour such as indigo-blue. Indigo has been used as a dye since the Middle Ages, when it was the only organic dye which gave a proper blue colour and wouldn't run. It is not like most other dyes, in that it is made from two plants, woad and the tropical indigo plant. Their leaves and branches contain a substance which, when treated in a complex process, takes on a deep blue colour. This process, which employs special techniques and equipment, is carried out by a body of craftsmen known as the 'blue dyers'. Huge quantities of indigo in small compact blocks are imported cheaply from Asia and the Americas.

The position of woad as a source of indigo was threatened by the indigo plant at the beginning of the sixteenth century – the age of discovery and of the building of colonial empires in the Indies and in America. The indigo plant produced a dye that was up to forty times more powerful than woad.

Indigo is produced in four stages.
The leaves and branches of the
indigo plant are steeped in large
pans filled with water. The next
stage is fermentation, which is
helped by the heat and humidity
of the tropical climate. The water
in the first pan is poured into a
second pan, where it is churned
around vigorously to oxygenate
it. This reaction with air converts
the colourless substance into an
indigo-blue liquid. Finally the
liquid is collected in a third pan in
which it evaporates, leaving a
solid residue of indigo.

The popularity of
indigo threatened the
livelihoods of European
farmers who grew
woad. Until 1737 its
use was strictly
forbidden in certain
Western countries, and
anyone found using it
could be given the death
penalty.

The Golden Gate

In 1848 the Gold Rush saw people swarm to San Francisco. In just a few months, prospectors from all over the world swelled this tiny village of a few hundred inhabitants into the largest town in California, with a population of 25,000 by the end of 1848. The town soon became rich, as every Sunday the gold-diggers rolled into town to gamble or drink away the treasure which they had painstakingly won from the riverbeds and mountainsides. But San Francisco was a miserable place in which to live. It was unhygienic, uncomfortable and dangerous, and there was no lighting, poor housing and little food. It was among this swarming mass of humanity that Levi Strauss chose to set up in business. Like most other wise shopkeepers and tradesmen, he was more interested in getting the prospectors to part with their gold than in finding any for himself.

Long before the Gold Rush, San Francisco was called the Golden Gate because of the yellow colour of the land and because it was situated in a bay at the foot of steep hills.

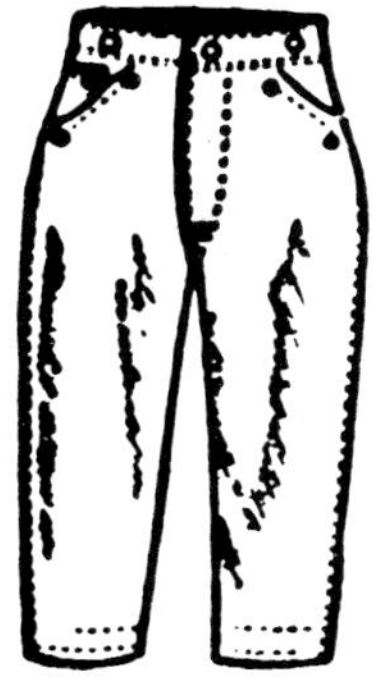

The pattern for the first pair of jeans (from 1853) shows a cut-off pair of dungarees with buttons for braces. Belt loops were not added to the waistband until 1922.

The Levi Strauss company's head office in San Francisco towards the end of the nineteenth century.

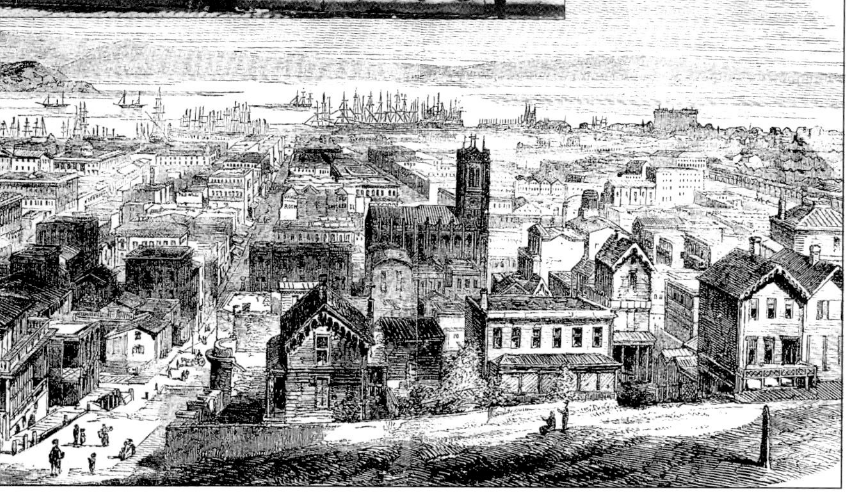

Today blue is the most popular colour with at least half the population of Western Europe. However, it was not until the end of the eighteenth century that it took over from red and became the colour and symbol of the Virgin Mary and of royal power.

The nomadic Touareg people are called the 'blue men' of the desert because of the blue marks left on their faces by the indigo dye from their blue 'chechia'. This is a long cotton scarf which is intricately wrapped around their heads to protect them from the sun and from the sand carried by the wind.

At the end of the nineteenth century and beginning of the twentieth, denim overalls were worn by working-class men. During the Second World War, however, American jeans manufacturers started to make them and they were worn only by men working for the American Ministry of Defence.

In an attempt to remove any distinguishing features between social classes in China, Mao Tse-tung encouraged every member of the most populated country in the world to wear identical blue suits.

There's gold in them thar hills

In 1848 thousands of men gave up
everything to go in search of gold. Soon
the news spread like wildfire and the
whole world went gold crazy: soldiers
deserted their barracks, factory workers
downed tools, sailors jumped ship and
farmers abandoned their fields.

How the West was won

The journey to California was a long and treacherous one. The 'forty-niners' (so called because they set out in 1849) made this journey into hell overland or by sea. When they arrived the would-be miners were exhausted, penniless and often in debt. They had sold everything when they left, packing the bare minimum into a trunk or wagon. Everyone who survived that ordeal, whether they had travelled as a family, in a group or alone, had experienced terrible suffering and sacrifice. But the dream captured the imagination of the world, and people came from all five continents in search of a better life. In a period of eight years, hundreds of thousands came to pit the steel of their pickaxes against the rock of the Sierra Nevada, to see it split open and gold flow out.

The first American star-spangled banner had thirteen red and white stripes and the same number of stars, symbolizing the original thirteen states which existed when the Declaration of Independence was signed in 1783.

The pioneers had to
contend with epidemics
and numerous accidents,
avoid drowning, and
put up with bad
weather, exhaustion
and lack of privacy.
Here a wagon train
crosses the prairie. It
was a journey of over
2,000 miles and had to
be organized with
almost military
precision.

The gold-diggers were not the only people who
wanted to emigrate to the New World. There
were also cattle-breeders, farmers and
shopkeepers. Few of them, however, got to
travel in comfort on the clippers. This was
because it was very expensive to travel on these
imposing sailing ships, first launched in 1851,
and also because steamships soon took their
place.

Trails across the New World

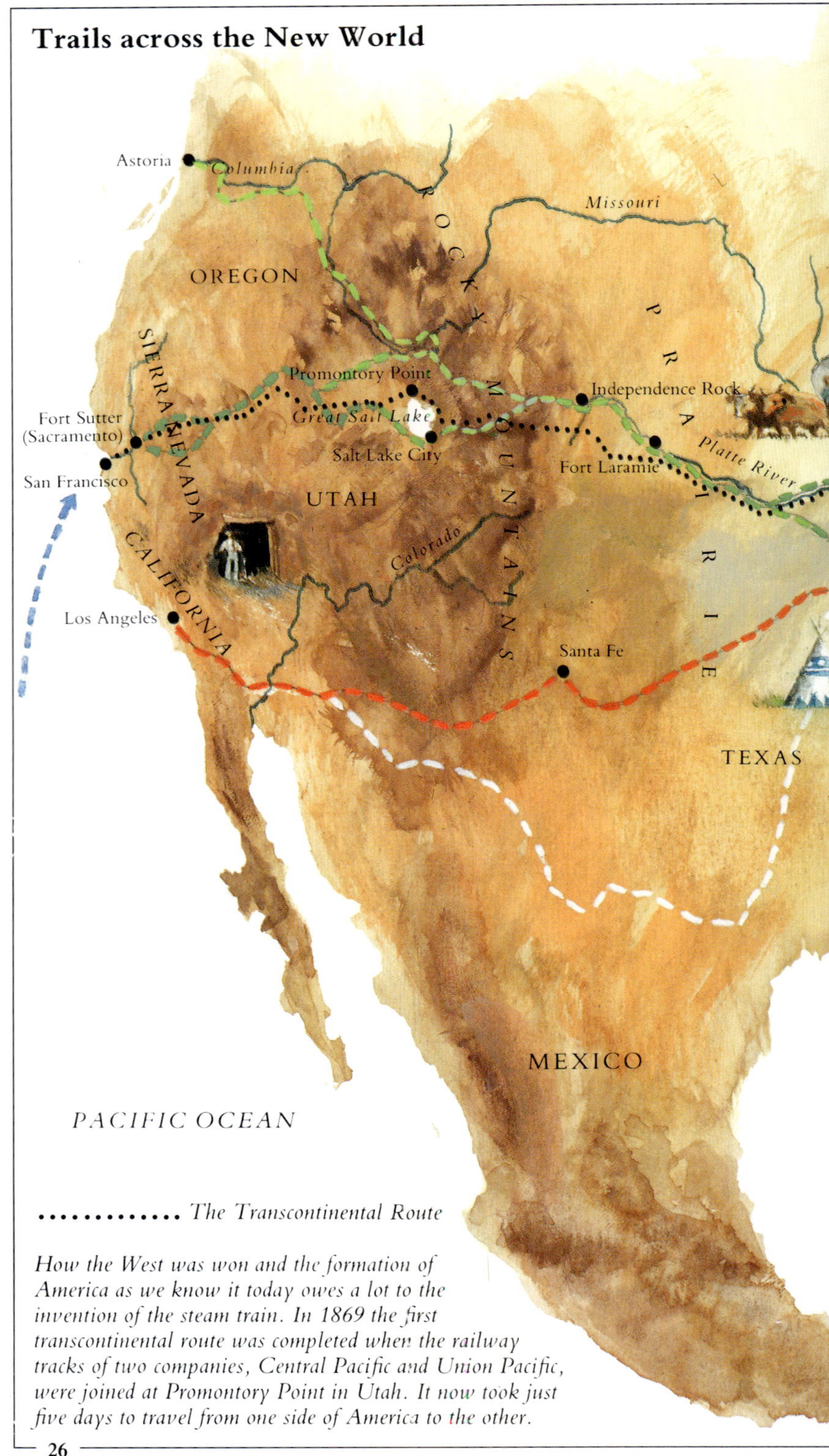

·············· *The Transcontinental Route*

How the West was won and the formation of America as we know it today owes a lot to the invention of the steam train. In 1869 the first transcontinental route was completed when the railway tracks of two companies, Central Pacific and Union Pacific, were joined at Promontory Point in Utah. It now took just five days to travel from one side of America to the other.

Three trails started from the east: the Oregon Trail and its alternative routes (green), the Santa Fe Trail (red), and a third trail which went through Mexico (white). It was also possible to reach California by sea via Cape Horn or by crossing the Panama isthmus (blue).

The reality of the gold-miner's dream
Up with the dawn, the gold-miner
leaves his makeshift camp to scour the
mountains and ravines. For fourteen to
sixteen hours a day he stands stooping in
freezing water, working himself to death
trying to divert the course of the river.
He builds dykes and dams so that he can
pan the sand of the old riverbed. He
frantically searches the sand in the hope
of finding some gold-dust or even a
nugget or two. But Lady Luck is cruel,
and more often than not the only thing
of any value that a miner possesses is his
equipment: a shovel, a pan, a pickaxe, a
donkey, a blanket, a knife, a frying-pan,
a few provisions and maybe a Colt 45.
He suffers terribly: from exhaustion,
scurvy, fever, alcoholism, injuries,
homesickness, isolation and depression.
The spirit of adventure doesn't last long –
just as long as it takes for the dream to
become a nightmare.

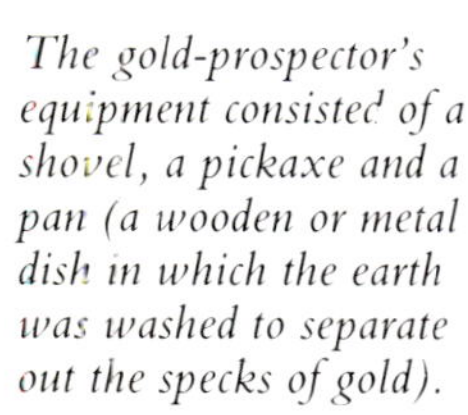

*The gold-prospector's
equipment consisted of a
shovel, a pickaxe and a
pan (a wooden or metal
dish in which the earth
was washed to separate
out the specks of gold).*

The methods used to extract gold changed after 1850, when the quality of tools improved. Tunnels were dug into the heart of the mountains using dynamite. The miners' clothes, however, didn't change at all. They continued to wear the same red flannel shirt, jeans and thick boots favoured by the pioneers.

In a period of eight years, more than 800 tonnes of gold were mined from the mountains of the Sierra Nevada. Everyone benefited: gold-prospectors saw their income increase tenfold, mining companies flourished, and the banks had tens of kilograms of the precious metal in their safes. (Nuggets this size were rare.)

Many of the towns of the West were either mushroom towns, because they sprang up out of the earth overnight, or ghost towns, because their inhabitants left as soon as there was no more gold to be found.

America! America!

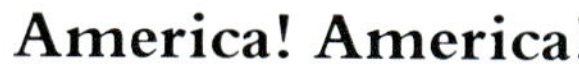

America became an economic
superpower at the beginning
of the twentieth century. Its
prosperity was founded on progress
and on the drive and ambition of its
people. When Levi Strauss died in
1902, he bequeathed to future
generations a pair of trousers
which were to acquire
mythical status.

Immigrants to the New World

In the course of the nineteenth century several million Europeans chose the United States as their new homeland. 170,000 people per year travelled there in the ten years between 1840 and 1850, and between 1890 and 1900 the figure rose to 370,000 per year. The tidal wave reached its peak in 1905, when over a million immigrants came to the New World. They were mostly from Britain, Italy, Poland and Russia, but people also came from China and Japan to work on the building of the railway lines and later settled on the West Coast. They all hoped to benefit from the incredible boom which had turned the United States into the biggest industrial nation in the world. The pioneers gave way to businessmen, and high finance took the place of high adventure. Huge fortunes were made. The dollar was king.

The beating heart of America was no longer the Great Plains, from where the Indians had now all been driven away, but the Atlantic ports and the industrious cities of the north-east: New York, Philadelphia, Pittsburgh, Detroit and Chicago.

'New York harbour, where all the shipwrecked people from the old world come ashore. Shipwrecked people, the wretched and the unhappy. Free men, soldiers on the run. People who have suffered misfortunes, people who have risked everything, people gripped by a romantic ideal.' (From L'Or (Gold) by Blaise Cendrars)

The immigration department was based on Ellis Island, New York, opposite the Statue of Liberty presented by France in 1886. Before setting foot on American soil, each immigrant had to undergo medical examinations and be interviewed by the police.

Far from quiet on the Western Front

Not all the pioneers who went West returned to jobs in workshops and factories. After the Gold Rush many of them took up farming and cattle-rearing. In the twenties many farmers started wearing jeans as everyday work clothes because they were so hard-wearing. The Wall Street Crash in 1929 devastated the urban and industrial areas of the East. In the space of two days there were countless bankruptcies and thousands of people were made redundant. Where else to turn to for a new start but the West, a land still haunted by the myth of the great adventurers? City-dwellers were attracted by the look and durability of jeans during this 'back to the farm' movement and took them home with them in their suitcases. Back in the cities, jeans became an original and even smart fashion item. A whole new group of customers had been created for the Levi Strauss company.

The first Levi's advertisements proclaiming the new 'Western fashion' were seen in 1935. Women were not left out: Lady Levi's were introduced three years later.

Because of the harsh economic situation, many well-off families had to give up their expensive holidays in Europe. Instead they went to ranches, where they enjoyed the cowboy lifestyle. In just a few years jeans acquired thousands of new fans.

In 1933 President Roosevelt instigated the New Deal, which consisted of a series of economic and social measures aimed in particular at farmers. They would receive state subsidies in return for reducing their output.

War and peace

Thanks to the Depression in 1929, jeans had suddenly become very popular and had effectively made the same journey as the pioneers but in reverse. The blue denim trousers were to become even more popular with the coming of the Second World War.

The Levi Strauss company signed an agreement with the American Ministry of Defence to manufacture the off-duty uniform of the US Navy Marines. This uniform was in fact a darker and slightly modified version of 501s. This exceptional order (several tens of thousands of pairs of trousers) won jeans their first stripes.

After the Allies' victory, jeans invaded Europe along with all the other wonderful consumer products only available in America, such as chewing-gum, Virginia cigarettes and Coca Cola. GIs became unexpected ambassadors for jeans.

When the soldiers returned home, American surplus stores continued to sell all these products. Soon the demand became too great and a black market started up. Jeans had conquered Europe and were here to stay. Quite an irony for the humble fabric from Nîmes.

25 August 1944, the liberation of Paris by the Allies. The people's joy, after five long years of deprivation, was unconfined.

The Marshall Plan, which was drawn up in June 1947, was intended to help the economic recovery of those European countries which had been ravaged by the war. It was financed almost entirely by the United States. In fifteen years more than 15,000 million dollars were given to the United Kingdom, France and West Germany. The money was a life-raft for these countries but also helped to boost American exports.

The stuff of heroes

After the Second World War, America continued to grow as an economic power against a background of political and moral austerity. But at the same time great changes were taking place in the cinema. Although many Hollywood films still offered dreams and escapism, some also tried to show the world the way it really was. Great directors like John Ford and Howard Hawks made hugely popular westerns, which portray a tough world where the cowboy is king. Other film-makers, such as Elia Kazan, depicted urban jungles with all their tensions and dramas.

New heroes were made with whom young Americans could identify: Marlon Brando (*The Wild Bunch, On the Waterfront*) and especially James Dean (*East of Eden, Rebel Without a Cause*). Naturally teenagers wanted to look like their screen idols, yet jeans were banned in schools because teachers associated them with immoral behaviour.

Women started wearing jeans in large numbers at the beginning of the sixties. Marilyn Monroe made them seem like the sexiest trousers around.

Gary Cooper in The Westerner *(1940). He was the archetypal cowboy, dressed in tough blue denims.*

James Dean in Rebel Without a Cause *(1955), in which a teenager from a good family rebels against the conformity of American society in the fifties.*

Rock 'n' roll attitude

At the same time as fifties cinema was reflecting the rebellious mood of young Americans, rock 'n' roll came kicking and screaming into the world. On university campuses, huddled around radios and juke-boxes, boys and girls were excited by the warm, deep voice of a young man called Elvis Presley. With 'That's All Right Mama' in 1954 he became the face and the body of rock 'n' roll. Especially the body: his swaying hips and fancy footwork would later get him tried for obscenity. However, many people reacted with distrust to this subversive music which had its roots in black culture. Although ignored at first by radio and television, things soon changed when Elvis was joined by other famous rock 'n' roll stars such as Bill Haley (*Rock Around the Clock*), Gene Vincent, Little Richard, Buddy Holly and Eddie Cochran. That's when the party really got started.

Chuck Berry, nicknamed 'Crazy Legs'. An excellent singer and guitarist, he was also a fine songwriter ('Johnny B. Goode', 'Sweet Little Sixteen').

The vinyl record, which first appeared after the Second World War, did much to popularize rock 'n' roll. Glittering juke-boxes became the focal points of bars and cafés.

With over 700 songs recorded and 600 million records sold by the time he died, Elvis Presley, the King, remains the universal symbol of rock 'n' roll.

What do you wear to a protest?
In the sixties in America jeans became
identified with all types of struggle:
racial, cultural and political. For
instance, as part of their campaign for
equal rights, blacks symbolically did not
wear their smart clothes when they went
to church on Sunday but wore jeans
instead. Native Americans today march
to assert their rights wearing the same
type of trousers as the pioneers who
drove out their ancestors. In 1968,
students opposed to the Vietnam war
took the university campuses and even
the lawns of the White House by storm.
Naturally they wore jeans. At about the
same time, someone had the idea of
widening the bottoms of these famous
trousers and tens of thousands of hippies
started wearing jeans as well. All these
minority groups were armed with just
one weapon: a pair of blue jeans.

Angela Davis, a black activist, describes the America of the sixties in this way: 'I lived for several years in Birmingham, Alabama, where I was brought up; we boycotted the racist stores with some success . . . In order to protest against the racism of the white storeholders, the black people put away their smart clothes and wore jeans to church. For a long time black people didn't buy any new clothes, as a protest against racial discrimination. At that time there was a very clear link between jeans and black people's struggle for freedom.'

Indigo-coloured jeans eventually succeeded in winning over people of all colours.

An A–Z of jeans

Until the sixties, the design of jeans did not change at all. The standard to aim at remained 501s, and other competing brands simply copied them in a series of virtually identical versions. It was the hippie movement which allowed jeans to show their true colours. They were widened, rolled up, fitted with zips, made to look like horse-riders' trousers, torn, patched together, worn threadbare, embroidered, etc. Soon a whole new vocabulary was invented. Jeans can be: 'natural', i.e. blue; 'bleached', when treated with chlorine; 'black', when the indigo thread is replaced by black thread; 'stonewashed', when they are washed in a machine with pumice stones which remove the colour in places and soften the fabric; 'used', when, after being stonewashed, the jeans are rubbed with sand to make them look old. The same result is achieved as if they had been worn every day for at least a year! But, above all, jeans are an essential fashion item for all young people in the world with a spirit of adventure.

Lee was the first brand to compete with Levi Strauss and was created in 1889. Wrangler dates from after the Second World War (1947), when sales of jeans were booming throughout the world.

Hippies were determined supporters of 'the American way of life' and lovers of freedom. Their trademarks were their unkempt hair, flowery tattoos and embroidered jeans. Between 1967 and 1973 they travelled all over the world and, of course, so did their jeans.

501s   Bell-bottoms   Embroidered flares

With zips   Baggy   Jodhpur style

Black   Punk style   Frayed

Jeans were for a long time considered by the Communist regimes in Europe to be a symbol of capitalist decadence. In these times of 'perestroika', however, and with the fall of the Berlin Wall, jeans are beginning to conquer the East too.

Contrary to what Westerns lead you to believe, not all cowboys were white. Blacks and Mexicans made up a third of these lonely and silent men. Cowboys were proud, and at first they shunned jeans because they were so popular with farmers, day labourers and slaves. Later, however, they made them their own, and jeans became the traditional costume worn at rodeos.

Further information

Working clothes called bib overalls, direct descendants of jeans, were created in about 1890. They are so called because they were often worn over other clothes. They were made in a variety of colours. Blue denim overalls were meant for people who worked outdoors, such as cowboys, labourers and boatmen. Striped overalls or overalls with a black and white or blue and white check were popular with lumberjacks, farmers and technicians. Those made from white fabric were suitable for house-painters, interior decorators, waiters, barmen and butchers.